TO: Aiden Bess

lots of love —
Sylvia

WITNESS

WITNESS

Karen Hesse

SCHOLASTIC INC.

New York Toronto London Auckland Sydney
Mexico City New Delhi Hong Kong Buenos Aires

The author and editors gratefully acknowledge
the Walter Dean Myers photograph collection,
and the families of Edith and Herbert Langmuir, Dean Langmuir,
and Joan Lacovara, for permission to use their photographs
to portray the characters depicted herein.

The characters portrayed in this book are fictitious
and not intended to represent specific persons living or dead.

12 11 10 9 8 7 6 5 4 3 2 1   3 4 5 6 7 8/0

Printed in the U.S.A.   40

First Scholastic paperback printing, January 2003

Original hardcover edition designed by Elizabeth Parisi,
published by Scholastic Press, September 2001

With sincere thanks to
the staffs at the Brattleboro and Springfield, Vermont, libraries;
to Randy, Kate, and Rachel Hesse; to Bernice Millman;
to Liza Ketchum, Eileen Christelow, Bob and Tink MacLean, and Wendy Watson;
and to Liz Szabla and Elizabeth Parisi.

To Jean Feiwel

And in this yard stenogs, bundle boys, scrubwomen,

sit on the tombstones, and walk on the grass of

graves, speaking of war and weather, of babies,

wages and love.

from "Trinity Peace"
by Carl Sandburg

The Characters...

Leanora Sutter (aged 12)

Percelle Johnson,
town constable (aged 66)

Sara Chickering,
farmer (aged 42)

Fitzgerald Flitt,
doctor (aged 60)

Harvey Pettibone, shop owner,
husband of Viola (aged mid-50s)

Merlin Van Tornhout (aged 18)

Esther Hirsh (aged 6)

Johnny Reeves,
clergyman (aged 36)

Iris Weaver, restaurant owner
and rum runner (aged 30)

Viola Pettibone,
shop owner (aged mid-50s)

Reynard Alexander,
newspaper editor (aged 48)

Setting: Vermont
Time: 1924

ACT ONE

leanora sutter

i don't know how miss harvey
talked me into dancing in *the fountain of youth*.
i don't know how she knew i danced at all.
unless once, a long time ago, my mamma told her so.

but she did talk me into dancing.
i leaped and swept my way through *the fountain of youth*
separated on the stage from all those limb-tight white girls.

    the ones who wouldn't dance with a negro,
    they went home in a huff that first day,
    but some came back.
    they told miss harvey they'd dance,
    but they wouldn't
    touch any brown skin girl.

only the little girl from new york,
esther,
that funny talking kid,
only esther didn't mind about me being colored.

merlin van tornhout

i pushed the window up in school
to get the stink of leanora sutter out of the classroom
where miss harvey brought her to show off
a dance from last week's
recital.

mr. caldwell
chuffed his arms,
faked a shiver,
ramped the sash back down
saying the day was too cold to leave a window open.

leanora sutter
turned and stared through me
    that witchy girl
    with those fuming eyes
she meant to put a curse on me.
she meant to.

i left school right then.
no amount of air will get the smell of her
out of my nose,
the soot of her out of my eyes.

esther hirsh

i did first meet sara chickering
when i had comings here last year
to be a fresh air girl in vermont.

vermont is a nice place.
they have wiggle fish.
that is what i did tell daddy in new york
when i had comings back to him.
i did ask daddy
to have our livings in vermont with sara chickering

for keeps.

but daddy did say no.

so i made a long walk all by myself.
i did follow the train tracks and
pretty quick daddy did have comings after me.

sara chickering made two rooms to be for us
in her big farmhouse
with her dog jerry.
we have sitting every night at the round table, next to the hot stove.
and i do catch the wiggle fish through
a hole sara chickering does make in the ice.

daddy gives helps when
sara chickering has needs for extra big hands.
but daddy is a shoe man. he has shoe knowings.
my friend sara chickering, she has knowings of all things else.

leanora sutter

in school willie pettibone handed me an article
torn from the town paper.
it said:

> *any person to whom an evening of hearty laughter is poison*
> *had better keep away from the community club minstrel show*
> *friday evening at the town hall. all others will be admitted*
> *for a night of fun brought to you by 22 genuine*
> *black-faced "coons."*

felt like skidding on ice as i read,
felt like twisting steel.

why can't folks just leave me alone?

daddy says:
how alone you want to be, leanora?
you're already nothing but a wild brown island.

percelle johnson

roads were bad.
don't blame me.
it's not my fault.
these roads are nothing but hog wallow during a thaw.
folks ought to know that.

wright sutter should have thought
before bringing his wife and child along to town with him.
that wasn't my fault,
his horse and wagon miring down,
stuck in the mud.
i wasn't even on duty.
not my fault he couldn't get help.
no one too energetic about helping a colored man hereabouts,
even if he is a neighbor.
sutter, making deliveries, left his womenfolk in the wagon too long.
wife took a chill,
waiting. she put her wrap around the little girl,
leanora.
sick all year, sutter's wife was. doc flitt said
she ought to go away to a sanatorium to get her health back.
wright sutter didn't have money for that.
even if there was a sanatorium for colored folk.
the sutter woman died this past spring.

don't blame me.
the roads were bad.

esther hirsh

the preacher man
johnny reeves
did have sittings on the riverbank
where i do make the leaves and
twigs float by in the ice green water.
even with my hat down over my ears i did hear him cry,
neighbor,
oh neighbor.
so i made my way to see what he did want.

johnny reeves did stand when he had seeings of me
and a girl did stand up in the brown tangle bank beside him and run away
and johnny reeves did yell
and make fist shakings at me
and i did yell
and make fist shakings back
and we did have a good game of yellings and shakings

until sara chickering did call me
and i had runnings back to the house
to gather the warm chicken eggs
from the steamy straw nests.

leanora sutter

they made me mad.
willie pettibone and some of the other boys, they said things
about me and daddy.

i shouldn't let them get to me but
i'm flint quick these days.

willie said:
    at the klan meeting last night
    the dragons talked about lighting you
    and your daddy up
    to get them some warmth on a cold day.
    you'd be cheap fuel, they said.
    they liked the smell of barbecue, they said.

i turned my back on willie pettibone and walked out of school.
i didn't know where i was going.
i just walked out
without my coat,
without my hat or rubbers.
i didn't feel the cold,
i was that scorched.

sara chickering

the day was cold,
bitter, below-zero.
made-you-wish-you'd-been-born-inside-a-fur-coat
      cold.
heavy sky, early dark, lamps already lit.
esther playing in the kitchen with her clothespin dolls,
and mr. hirsh still at the shoe store. that's
when leanora sutter, half frozen,
showed up on my porch.

she wore no coat, her head was bare, no rubbers on her feet,
nothing but worn-thin school clothes standing between her
      and the teeth of winter.
i brought her in.
sat her on a chair by the stove.
put a mug
      the chipped one
of warm broth in her hands.

esther dragged my best quilt into the kitchen and
worked it up over leanora's shoulders.
only esther would go lugging out the company best
for a colored girl.

i left leanora there with esther,
ran the half mile to iris weaver's restaurant
      with the coffee flowing and the politics raging around me
phoned doc flitt and constable johnson,
let them know i had leanora and she wasn't in any too good shape,
and they'd better hurry along.

constable johnson said he'd go after the girl's father.
make sure wright sutter got his child home safe and sound
to that little place they rent from lizzie stockwell
out the west end of town.
constable said he didn't want happening to leanora,
what happened to the mother.

when i got back to the house,
esther sat at leanora's feet,
little round esther leaning against
that slender brown girl, with her long head and longer limbs.
gave me some turn
seeing those two motherless children
    in my kitchen
    before the stove,
esther's hair draped across leanora's lap,
leanora's dark hand stroking esther's silk face.

after wright sutter drove away with leanora,
i looked at the empty chair by the stove,
the quilt still slung over it, spilling onto the floor.

i never had a colored girl in my kitchen before.

leanora sutter

i told daddy i wasn't going back to school.
daddy said:
of course you are.
no low-down white boy's gonna stop leanora sutter
from getting an education.

johnny reeves

some preacher down south
has himself a following
of coloreds
and whites,
together.
they trail after him from town to town,
forgetting their duties to home.

they even tried him, neighbor, they tried him
before a jury of white men
for inciting trouble,
for leading the lord's sheep to stray,
and still, neighbor, it grieves me to tell you that
still,
they let the devil go free.

it's a sorry state, neighbor,
it's a pitiful state of affairs when a colored preacher
can lure good white folk from their hearths.

leanora sutter

my daddy says
down in texas
a reverend by the name of
revealed jesus
is preaching so powerful,
people are leaving their jobs and their houses and
following him from meeting to meeting.

my daddy says
revealed jesus better get his brave behind up north pretty quick because
what he's doing down there in texas
is sure to get him lynched.

johnny reeves

oh, neighbor.
down in that den of the devil,
down in that center of sin,
down in new york's harlem,
negroes kill other negroes
    over gambling debts,
    over women,
    over gin.

hear me, neighbor.
if we are patient,
if we are patient, my good neighbor,
we can stay here at home,
we can take care of our problems at home
and down there in harlem, the
negro problem will
    settle
    itself.

esther hirsh

in new york
i did see someone whose poor head
did have a bullet inside it
and he did
have blood everywhere in the street
where he did sleep so still.

daddy and sara chickering did talk at the table.
a man with the name of senator greene did get a bullet in his head, too.
i did make a whisper sound
to hear this talk.
    like birds falling.
daddy did say
don't cry esther. senator greene is getting better again.
daddy says bullets are a very bad thing.
but daddy says
sometimes you can even get a shooting in the head
and still be okay.
sara chickering did say yes that is true.
so it has to be.

percelle johnson

the ku klux klan
is looking to rent the town hall for their meetings.
why shouldn't they?

iris weaver

some girls i know have gone out in the world.
but most have married,
settled down to
children
and housework.
i'm different.
i have this restaurant.
i have a secret life, too.
a life the law is forever dogging me over.

i run booze.

i know every foot of ground
between boston and montreal.
i could walk the distance blindfolded.
i know the names of the customs officers,
american and canadian,
where they're stationed,
what shift they're on,
the tough ones,
and the ones who can't resist a pretty leg
or a slice of apple pie.

the officers in vermont are the toughest.
i've brought loads through highgate and alburg,
but mostly i go through new york:

rouses point and plattsburg.
i drive a good secondhand packard.
it has plenty of pep,
plenty of room to carry a load.

and it's got damn good springs.

johnny reeves

have you seen the way the girls dance?
sinful, neighbor, sinful.
these girls
doing the unspeakable gyrations of satan.
with each step they unravel the
moral fiber of our country.

they must be stopped.
not by law, neighbor,
not by legislation. this is no business of the government.
it is up to us, neighbor.
it is up to us to lock our daughters in
until they learn to behave,
until we destroy in them
the wanton will of satan.

fitzgerald flitt

the flapper
is not the least bit alarming,
nor a sign of the declining social standard.
though she drinks cocktails and shows an inordinate fondness
for lipstick and the rouge pot,
we have nothing to fear.

i doctor these women
and i have seen over the last years a transformation in them.
and what i see,
        the opening of roses kept bud-tight so many years,
it warms this aging soul.

sara chickering

they say maple sugar
is becoming as old-fashioned
as the paisley shawl,
but to see esther hirsh suck on a lump,
her face star-blissed with
sweet delight,
i think that old-time maple,
it's still all right.

harvey and viola pettibone

harvey says:
the ku klux are here, vi.
there's not a thing to stop them. we might as well join them.
why not?
they're not low-down, like some folks say.
they're good men,
100 percent american men.
and they might bring us some business.

viola says:
in texas, harvey,
those "good" men thought a certain fella was
keeping company with a married lady.
they had no proof of hanky-panky, harv.
they beat him, anyway,
held a pistol to his head,
said they'd kill him if he didn't clear out.
harv, you don't want to join a group like that.

but harvey says:
that's just rumor.
they have parades, vi,
and picnics,
and speakers from all over.
wouldn't you like that?
picnics and speakers?

viola washes up the dinner dishes,
her hands gloved in soapy water.

they do good, vi. they take care of their women.
and liquor can't ever tear up a family with them around.

harvey examines a spot on one of the glasses.
shouldn't we join, vi?

viola shakes her head slowly back and forth.
no, harv, viola says. i don't think we should.

reynard alexander

this paper is neutral.
this editor is neutral.
i have attempted to remain neutral
in the face of the klan question
and i intend to continue neutral
until i have reason
to do otherwise.

leanora sutter

teacher says lewis won't be coming back to school.
he got himself killed yesterday
playing in the sandbank. it
buried him.
he was alone.
lewis was always alone,
down in that sandbank,
making big sand cities
that he limped away from when his ma
called him home for dinner,
big sand cities willie pettibone and those boys
came in and wrecked
so lewis'd have to start again.
this time the sand slid right down on top of lewis
and buried him
in the very city he was building.

i am being buried, too,
in all this whiteness.

iris weaver

well how do you like that.
down in texas,
mrs. miriam ferguson,
the wife of the impeached governor,
defeated the klan candidate
by 80,000 votes
to win the democratic nomination for her state.

if she wins,
she'll be the first woman
governor in
this whole damn country.

imagine.

harvey and viola pettibone

if we join the klan, harvey says,
we can wipe out bronson's grocery by next year, vi.
all the klan members will shop here,
even if they live closer to bronson.
bronson's made his feelings against the klan clear.
if we join up with them, how long could bronson last? six months, nine?

viola says:
and what about all our regulars, harv?
we make this store "klan only"
we lose a lot of business.
where do you think they'll all go?

harvey says:
it doesn't matter. that little bit of business,
it won't be enough to keep bronson flush, vi. you'll see.

i don't think so, viola says.

sara chickering

folks ask why i never married.
i watched my
father swallow his breakfast whole and rush away,
leaving mother with us children to be readied for school,
lunch to be prepared for noon,
washing to be done,
and the fitting out of a big evening meal.

father would come home late,
tired out,
falling asleep in the best chair after supper,
while mother put the house to rights,
got me, my brothers, my sister
and, finally, father off to bed.

from morning until night,
every day of the week,
that was mother's life.
father got a holiday from time to time.
mother never did.

that's why i moved out and came to work on the farm.
soon as i could i bought it for my own.
all these years i've managed fine without a man.
i may work as hard as my mother,
but i'm drudge to no one.

johnny reeves

we shall reign in the kingdom,
neighbor.
we shall form a great fist,
and we shall still those who oppose us.
we shall strike them out,
wipe them out,
blot them out.
together we cast a long shadow, neighbor,
and with our shadow
we cast our foes in darkness.
we cast those who are not like us into the arms of satan.

every one of the lord's lambs wants the light shining on him,
neighbor,
every lamb can see the right way when he is
standing in the light of the lord.
every lamb, once he has known the light,
cannot endure the darkness.
come stand with me in the light, neighbor.

ACT TWO

leanora sutter

there was a boy in chicago,
a rich boy.
he was kidnapped.
the kidnappers wanted $10,000
from the boy's daddy
to bring the boy back alive.
only he was already dead.
even before the ransom note came,
the boy was already dead,
naked in a ditch, miles away from his house.
that boy was fourteen.
and now he's dead.
and he was rich.
and he was white.

esther hirsh

my brain did get hurt yesterday.
doc flitt says
it did get hurt a little like senator greene.

i was having chasing games with margaret
and i did fall and hit my head on a rock.
the rock made big heart beatings in my eye.
i did find my way home to sara chickering
with the good dog jerry helping me
but i didn't feel any good feelings anywhere.
and then my eyes did see only darks
and i did get confused and
thinkings i did drown in sand
the way lewis did with his lame leg.
and then lewis did take my hand
and he gave me showings of the way back home
to my nice little bed in sara chickering's house.

this morning i did wake up
and my brain is all good feelings again.
and i can have seeing again and the darks is all gone
and the big heart beatings is just a little thump thumps.

doc flitt says
i am like senator greene
only i did get better so much faster.

percelle johnson

the chicago police did it.
they solved the case of that murder
of fourteen-year-old bobby franks.
it was the spectacles that
led detectives to the slayers.

nathan leopold, jr.,
    son of a millionaire manufacturer,
and richard loeb,
    his companion,
were taken into custody
for kidnapping and killing their neighbor.

the reports say both leopold and loeb are smart,
students at the university in chicago.
they made full confessions to the charges,
said they'd been planning the job
since november.

if leopold had not dropped his spectacles,
if the spectacles had not been so uncommon,
they would have gotten away with it.
they would have gotten away
    with murder.

merlin van tornhout

it took two of them
my age
to kill one skinny jew boy.
two of them.
planning every detail.
they rented an automobile, killed the kid,
dumped the body, buried the boots and belt buckle
in different places.
they planned for weeks to kidnap,
to kill.
to see how it felt.
to prove they could.
it didn't matter about jail,
or being haunted by a ghost,
didn't even matter about going to hell.

if i wanted to, i could kill someone all by myself.
wouldn't need anyone's help,
and i'd make damn sure i got some money for my trouble.
but they were rich jew kids.
what do you expect?

sara chickering

caught a
german
carp
just below
the falls.
measured
two
and
one-half
feet and weighed
37 pounds.

caught it on
plain old
silk line.

esther helped.

leanora sutter

my daddy said mr. field, the uncle of miss stockwell, our landlady,
was feeling poorly
and i might take myself over to see
if i could be of any use.

when i got there i washed up his dishes
and swept his floor
and boiled some potatoes for his supper.

while i worked he talked.
at first i didn't listen.
mr. field is a white man
with cheeks shrunk in enough to make his
ears and his eyes too big for the rest of his face.
and a neck so scrawny,
not a collar exists that could tighten around it.

he started in on war stories.
civil war.
he told me about being a bugler for his regiment.
but he said that didn't keep him out of danger.
he was standing right beside a colonel who was shot through the middle.

mr. field said: i saw the brigade of negroes under general burnside.
like a long streamer of dark silk they were.

he stared off through his wire spectacles,
the lenses so dirty
even if his eyes were clear
he couldn't have seen much.

they were a sight, he said.
that line of negroes,
marching toward the rebels,
straight as a dress parade.

what happened to them, i asked,
expecting nothing good.
mr. field said: why,
those negro soldiers chased the rebels out.
every one.

i made a pie for mr. field.
he kept talking.
i don't know if he could see me well enough
to judge the color of my skin.
i don't know if my color mattered one whit to him.
he just said:
you come by anytime, miss sutter.
you move nice and quiet
and you make my kitchen smell like it
did when i had a wife here. and i do
like a flaky apple pie.

i marched home in a straight line,
with my back tall,
and thought about that regiment of men
like a streamer of dark silk.

esther hirsh

when the barn cat did have her six little kittens
sara chickering had takings of the baby kittens
away from their mamma.

what did you do with the little things?
i did ask sara chickering.

sara chickering said the kittens did go far away.

that is what they said about my mamma, too. she did go
far away on the train to heaven.

will the kittens come back? i did ask.

no, sara chickering said. the kittens won't come back, esther.
if the kittens come back they will eat the birds.
if the birds are eaten they can't catch the bugs.
then the bugs will come and kill my crop.
that's why the kittens are gone.

i do like the little kittens. even when they are blind
and have no fur and move around like
pink baby tongues and smell like
warm rubber balls. i do like to watch them.

i did go along the railroad tracks to find where
sara chickering left the little kittens. i did think i could find them

before they had leavings on the train to heaven and
i could be their mamma and keep them in the woods
and make them eat only warm milk and biscuit.

but i could have no findings of the little kittens.

harvey and viola pettibone

hey, vi, harvey says.
did you know the average woman
is happiest when she prepares food in her own kitchen
and sits down with the family to enjoy it?

viola is cutting up chicken in the back room.
where'd you hear that, harv?

harvey says: johnny reeves was in the store
picking up groceries for old mrs. reeves.
he had a crowd gathered around him
and he was preaching. he said we'd all be better off if we
got the family
out of the restaurant
and back to the dinner table.
he said the average woman,
she loves her home and family first.
she might have got distracted
when she was earning wages
while her man fought in the great war.
but the trend is the other way now.

viola says:
was iris weaver in the store when he was doing this preaching?

harvey says:
no. matter of fact he waited until she left.

viola nods and smiles.
i guess he did.

sara chickering

it's not hard putting up with mr. hirsh.
he isn't like my father.

maybe since he's so young.

he washes dishes,
helps with chores,
he even does a turn at the stove every few days.

he bathes esther,
reads to her in all manner of voices,
makes us both laugh till our sides hurt.
he washes her clothes,
gets her to school and helps her with her homework.

best man i ever saw.

iris weaver

i know i shouldn't be running liquor.
and maybe i'll end up in jail.
but i paid for this restaurant
by transporting hooch
and i've made enough
to fork out tuition for two of my brothers
and my baby sister, who is smart as sateen,
and would have been trapped in this valley forever.

leanora sutter

when i was taking care of mr. field,
doing the light chores,
keeping him alive with my plain
cooking and housekeeping,
i told him about helen keller and how she was blind all the way
and how i wrote her a letter.
and he showed me a
remington portable typewriter,
almost new.

you have any use for that? he asked.
for your letter writing and all?

no sir, i said.

i would have liked a machine like that to write on.
but if i went carrying a big old
typewriter home from
dickenson street
all the way to
mather road,
constable johnson,
he'd get ten calls before i got halfway to the covered bridge,
telling him how the colored girl
stole some
expensive machinery.

not worth the trouble.

merlin van tornhout

mary said:
what about we get married, merle?
you're almost done with school,
you got that night job at the paper,
we could live on that.
come bust me out of this place, merle.

i like mary fine.
maybe enough to marry her.

but i don't know.

she wrote a letter to johnny reeves
asking if he'd do the ceremony and
if we could get married in ku klux robes,
with flowers embroidered over the fiery cross.
and johnny reeves said, yes.

but i never yet have
paid my 10 dollars to the klan.
and mary,
well, i don't know what the klan would make of her.
when she was still down here,
she bought all her shoes
from the jew store.

iris weaver

merlin van tornhout
just can't keep himself out of trouble.
with all the talk about
leopold and loeb
he goes driving off to
rescue his 15-year-old girlfriend
from an orphanage in burlington
and gets hauled into jail for kidnapping.

boy's got spirit, i'll give him that.
his girl told him she wanted out,
and he drove up there to spring her.

they were caught in vergennes,
mary placed in custody
of a policewoman,
merlin arrested and held in the lockup.

he should be back in a few days.
reynard alexander went and pitched for him.
it helps having reynard alexander for a friend.
i should know.

merlin van tornhout

constable johnson told me it'd be better
if i watched my step after the trouble
i got in
trying to help mary.

harvey and viola pettibone

did you have to buy so many, viola says,
looking at the stack of phonograph records.

harvey closes his eyes and breathes deeply.
when i go in the music store,
i want everything, he says.

viola says:
if you would only sit in the booth and try out half a dozen records
before you buy, you'd know exactly what
you're getting, you'd
get exactly
what you want.

harvey says:
i did get what i wanted. why should i spend half my life
squeezed inside a soundproof cubby,
when i can come home
and listen in peace in my own chair.

viola says:
we'll see how much peace you get, mr. pettibone.
i was hoping to put
new linoleum on the floor this month.
now it looks like we might just have to
nail your records down
instead.

johnny reeves

we took a pine
40 feet high and
lashed a cross arm
to it and set the
cross in the ground,
its arms stretching above the town. we soaked burlap bags
in kerosene and wrapped the bags around the wood.
at the foot of the
cross i smashed
a railroad torch.
the fire took off
so fast. a divine
sight, neighbor,
the flames spread
from the base to the
top. in a matter of
minutes the cross arm
pulsed with fire. the
flames leaping,
seeking heaven,
neighbor, the white
crucifix scoring
the night
blazed perfect.
perfect.

merlin van tornhout

i don't care what constable johnson says.
before i left for work,
i went up with johnny reeves and them
and we lit up prospect hill
with a fiery cross.
the kerosene took off so fast.
burned so fierce. christ.
i can still see it when i close my eyes.

leanora sutter

i woke up saturday night
because the light coming through
my bedroom window changed.

on the hill across the valley
i saw
a flame
rising.
but it was
no wild fire. it
was a
cross,
burning.

silently,
silently,
i crept down the hall,
into the closet
where,
at the back,
mamma's cotton dress
still dangled over her shoes,
and the walls smelled of hair oil and oranges.

in that dark and narrow place,
i opened a hole for myself
but no matter how i turned,
the light from the cross
curled its bright claws under the door.

reynard alexander

down in town,
families listened to the independence day concert,
while up on the hill a fiery cross was set ablaze.
it started burning about the time the band finished
    the star-spangled banner.

only a lunatic
would ignore the dry conditions,
or the fact that a crackling fire
could spread so easily out of control.

or perhaps it was the work of children
stirred by griffith's *birth of a nation*,
    that racist rubbish,
      which will not fade away.

esther hirsh

sara chickering did take me for a walk
on the other side of flat rock
from where the cross did burn
the other night.

sara chickering did grumble about men in their nightshirts
with their filthy wet hems
and i did laugh at her
    so serious
and ask her the names for all the flowers,
all the growing plants like
ebony spleenwort and
rusty woodsia.

as we did walk through the meadow
back to sara chickering's house
we did see flowers with more good names
like violet and saxifrage and cowslip,
and we did see birds with the most happy namings like
meadowlark
and bobolink
and savanna sparrow.
they did make a music in the shimmery air
and there were flickers and
orioles and
bluebirds turning circles.

and as i did look up to give thanks to sara chickering for all the namings,
a whippoorwill had singings
and the music did come from sara chickering's mouth.

iris weaver

i was born protestant.
but i'd join the catholic church
before
i'd throw my lot in with the klan.

sara chickering

i never thought much about it before.
if esther hadn't needed a place the last minute
with all those fresh air kids coming to town,
i never would think of it still.
i might have joined the ladies' klan.
become an officer, even.
klan can seem mighty right-minded, with their talk of family virtue,
mighty decent, if you don't scratch the surface.
there's a kind of power they wield,
a deceptive authority.

i think a lot about it these days.
the klan says they don't stand against anyone.
    but a catholic, a jew, a negro,
    if they got arrested,
    and the judge was klan,
    and the jury was klan,
    you can't convince me they'd get a fair trial.

it took having the hirshes here
to see straight through
to the end of it.

esther hirsh

someone did wrap a letter over a stone and they did send it
through sara chickering's kitchen window.
i have not knowings what the letter said.
daddy would not give readings of the words to me.
he did say a hiss word like steams coming from the teakettle
and make slow shakings of his head.
sara chickering,
when she did read the letter,
she made angry sayings.
    when sara chickering does get angry she is
    walking
    so fast,
    like a dog who has needs for squats.
    she does go so fast sparks are coming on the braided rug.
daddy did say he would sit at the table and not have sleeps.
sara chickering let me have sleeps in her bed.
daddy did say nobody not anybody not even klan is hurting little girls
and
i can have sleeps with no fearing.

i like
having sleeps with sara chickering
except it does make me
hungry in the hot night
when sara chickering is all
smelling
of spicy green tomatoes.

sara chickering

ira hirsh
saw in the paper
an ad for a flat on main street.
    five rooms,
        completely furnished.
he asked if he should take it.
get the klan to leave me alone.
i can't imagine life without that child under my feet,
asking a thousand questions
with that odd way of hers,
talking to the animals
and the plants
and the furniture
as if everything
was talking back.
i can't imagine life without that child.
i told mr. hirsh so in so many words.

damn klan.
to think of what they could drive from my life
with their filthy
little
minds.

ACT THREE

esther hirsh

sara chickering did come with me
and we did gather
sticks and sticks of rhubarbs from the garden.
we did put the rhubarbs in my wagon
and have squeaks, squeaks to town,
pulling the rhubarbs behind us all the places
and we did sell sara chickering's rhubarbs,
ten sticks a nickel.
and we had comings back with the rattle-empty wagon,
and five jingle nickels.

percelle johnson

caught iris weaver
with twenty bottles of bootleg whiskey in her car.
but the man she was with
said it was his hooch and iris didn't know what all she was carrying.
now i know it was iris running that booze,
but the gentleman's going to jail for her,
serving the sentence she ought to serve.
if you ask me,
a girl goes and bobs her hair and her head starts
filling with nothing but monkey business.

sara chickering

heard talk around town that
the hearse of a slain klansman
caught fire on its way to the cemetery.

what do you suppose the lord
was trying to say about that?

johnny reeves

neighbor,
as the hearse drove
past hundreds of persons
lining the sidewalks,
an act of god,
a thunderbolt
struck the car itself,
sparking it to
smoke and flames.

an act of god,
neighbor,
to express the lord's anger
that one
of his special children
had fallen.

reynard alexander

on arrival in a town,
the klan appears to serve the best interest of
the greater community,
"cleaning" it up, keeping a vigilant eye out for
loose morals and lawbreakers.
they deliver baskets to the needy,
and money to the destitute,
but the needy the klan comforts are white protestant needy,
the destitute white protestant, too.

a catholic with troubles, a negro, a jew, a foreigner?
their problems are of no concern to the klan.

from state to state,
from town to town,
men join who cannot be trusted.
      unscrupulous men
      who work in the dark
      behind hoods and masks.
it takes but ten dollars.

and when that sort of scoundrel
starts hiding under hood and robes,
no good can come of it.

johnny reeves

i have reached the pinnacle, neighbor.
tapped by the exalted dragons.
i, neighbor, led the klan
in their opening prayers.

the gathering prayed with me,
neighbor, in the summer morning
with the bees humming in the clover.
they prayed with me as i declared the klan a
movement of god.

heads uplifted, we offered ourselves to the almighty,
calling all
protestants
to band together
for the sake of home and country

and we sang

america.

leanora sutter

i was on my way up main street when i saw esther.
she was picking stands of dandelion, talking her strange talk
about birds and kittens, about lewis and
stopping the train
so she could take flowers to heaven and visit her mother.

i walked with her a while, listening,
then waved goodbye at the bottom of main street hill.
i hadn't gone far
when i heard the train whistle.
i couldn't see the tracks
or esther
but
    i saw my mother,
    running
and i
started running, too, toward her,
racing between buildings.

then my mother was gone, but there was esther,
looking up,
still as a rock,
gazing at
that big train,
rushing down on her,
expecting it to stop and let her on.

i pretty near flew

it didn't seem i could ever move fast enough
but i ran

as the whistle shrieked
as the brakes screamed
as the fireman crawled out onto the grinding locomotive.
the train was nearly on top of her when i leaped,
grabbed esther, and rolled her to safety,
locked in my arms,
the two of us cradled in a mess of seed and dandelion.

sara chickering

leanora sutter
snatched esther from the path of the maine central locomotive,
racing the engine while the fireman crawled out
in the hope of a rescue,
an impossible rescue.

they saw esther on the tracks.
set their brakes
but the train was so heavy,
it ran a quarter mile more
before
screeching
to a
stop.

in that wrenching stretch
the men were certain they'd killed her.

can't hardly think of anything
but leanora sutter
in my kitchen last winter, wrapped in my best quilt,
and yesterday, esther, wrapped in
leanora,
inches from the railroad tracks,
safe in a nest of dandelion.

esther hirsh

i do have the prickle scratches on my legs and on my arm
from where
leanora did push me down in the tangle grass
and sara chickering says in a big scold voice
that i am never, never, ever stopping a train
not ever, never, never on the train tracks.
but

i do miss my mamma and her summer
skin.

reynard alexander

wright sutter
received a letter
in the mail
warning him to leave town.

whoever wrote that letter said
they saw the article about leanora
saving the hirsh child from the train.
said,
they'd tie them both to the tracks next time,
make sure neither walked away.

fearing for leanora,
sutter took the letter to percelle johnson.

johnson
asked the head of the local klan what they knew about such threats.

klan said,
we didn't send it.

merlin van tornhout

put a colored girl in the paper,
call her a hero,
just cause she saved a kid
from being hit by a train.
a jew kid.

i could have saved the kid.
i saw it, too. that train
tearing along the track.
i saw it, too.

i didn't run like that colored girl did.
i didn't try.
maybe i was thinking no one could.
no one could beat that train.

but the colored girl,
i never saw anyone move so fast.
she ran like a deer,
like a deer in a rifle sight,
      one you let go
      cause there's no way to hit
      a swift brown rush weaving through the trees like that.

i'm not saying she did anything i couldn't have done,
but when i think on it,
maybe i didn't try because something,
something kept me in my place,
watching that colored girl run.

esther hirsh

bossie did stray from the pasture
into mr. hobart's garden
where she had eatings of all the good green stuffs
and she did have happy goings up and down the garden rows.
when mr. hobart had wakings up,
he did see our bossie
in his garden,
and he did take his gun and fire at
bossie.

bossie is a smart cow
and right away she had runnings home to us.
the animal doctor did make a good promise that
bossie does not ever have the living coming out of her.
and i am having big glads to hear this
because i do like it better to play with
bossie with the living in her.

fitzgerald flitt

some klansmen, goosed on bootleg whiskey, broke
into the basement
of the roman catholic cathedral in burlington
expecting to find
tanks and guns,
airplanes and acid,
ammunition enough to level new england.

all they found was dust,
some worn vestments,
and a dented chalice,

which they stole.

reynard alexander

what is the ku klux klan?
is it the patriotic organization it claims to be?
100 percent americans.
what is a 100 percent american?
what of catholics, jews, negroes,
citizens of any other race or color born here,
whose fathers were born here,
and grandfathers.
are they not every bit as 100 percent american as the klan?

viola pettibone

i accompanied oscar scott to the train station
to meet john philip sousa
and bring him to the auditorium
to play with his band of eighty musicians.
i handed mr. sousa a bouquet of flowers and
the key to the city,
which he accepted grandly.

the band played nine numbers though they
had just three hours here in town.
they gave a full concert,
and a number of encores,
all mr. sousa's compositions.

they saved for last
stars and stripes forever
and took the house by storm.

harvey held a seat for me.
but
i watched the concert from the wings,
as mr. sousa's guest.

percelle johnson

viola pettibone, who mothers that cat of hers
the way only viola pettibone can,
found her maltese stuck way up in the crotch of a tree
on the bank leading down to the railroad track.

she tried coaxing it out,
tried getting her boy willie to go after it, but that boy's good for nothing,
and her customers wouldn't climb that tree.
danged cat.
pretty near everyone with a place backing the river came out,
vexed from listening to it yowl.

guess it was scared 60 feet up in the air,
too scared to consider coming down on its own and no one
willing to go up after it.

fire department came.
they sized up the scene and
called me.

i wasn't going up in my uniform.
pulled on a pair of overalls,
placed a ladder against the lowest part of the tree.
12 feet i covered that way.
the remaining 48 had to be shinnied up,
one inch at a time in the pouring rain.

blasted cat wouldn't come.
not even when i reached it.
i tried sweet talking it into letting go of the bark.

finally had to pry it loose,
put the thing on my shoulder, its claws stabbing into my back.

slowly we came down.
6 feet from the ground the cat ripped my shirt, climbed my face
and leaped
into viola's arms.

put my uniform back on and wrote up a ticket, handing it to
harvey pettibone
next time, i said,
keep your cat to home.

fitzgerald flitt

mr. clarence darrow,
the lawyer defending those chicago boys,
believes
that under no circumstances
should the state take a
human life.
that's why he's shouldering this case.
the guilt of leopold and loeb,
the two young murderers of bobby franks,
is without question.
it is darrow's intention
not to prove their innocence,
but to cheat the hangman
    in spite of their guilt.
and perhaps in so doing
remove the underpinnings
of every gallows across this land.

a civilized man in america.
how refreshing.

reynard alexander

leopold and loeb
who had stuck together
through the hearing,
snickering and laughing
as they moved to and from the courtroom,

sat silently,
avoiding each other
as they heard for the first time,
their separate confessions read aloud
each accusing the other of
stunning young franks with a chisel
and snuffing out his life.

esther hirsh

i did watch with daddy at the railroad tracks this morning
as the circus had their summer comings. daddy did keep a tight
hold on my hand and he did tell me again the ways of trains
while the circus people did roll their big wagons
off the flat cars.
they did have elephants pushing the wagons
and horses pulling.

all the circus people and animals
had knowings of the job they must do.
men and men with big hammerings.
tent poles did stand up so quick
and a cookhouse did nearly put itself together
with breakfast sizzling inside it
pancakes and fried eggs flipping
and that good breakfast smell filling the meadow
        the same as is always in sara chickering's kitchen.

by the time sara chickering did come to get me
the big tent did fill the meadow
and the smaller tents did look like spiderwebs
traced in raindrops.

sara chickering and i did rush to watch the parade pass by
        on main street.
we did see lions and tigers,
hippos and kangaroos,
monkeys and zebras and bears,
and the beautiful ladies in their sparkly clothes,
and acrobats and tightrope walkers and clowns

who did make us laugh as they flopped past
in their big shoes
and i did tell sara chickering we must be bringing those clowns to
    daddy
so he can give them better fittings for their feet.

merlin van tornhout

i've had this job with the paper nearly six months now,
working the hours after the night men leave,
before the day men come on and i have to
get to school.

the klan doesn't think much of the paper.
or its editor.
but mr. alexander,
he gave me this job,
he got me out of jail,
he made a set of three keys: the back door, the storeroom, the truck.
no one ever trusted me like that before.

i could climb pretty high with the klan, handing them those keys,
but i wouldn't do it.
they'd use those keys,
i don't know what for.

reynard alexander

clarence darrow pleaded for the life of leopold and loeb. he said:

> *why did they kill little bobby franks?*
> *not for money.*
> *not for hate.*
> *they killed him*
> *because somewhere*
> *in the infinite processes*
> *which go into the making of the boy or the man,*
> *something slipped.*

something has slipped
not only in chicago.
something has slipped in towns everywhere across america,
in maine and in kansas,
in oregon and indiana and vermont,
something has slipped and as a result
we are all
sliding
back toward the dark ages.

johnny reeves

nathan leopold, jr.
scratched out his last will
and testament, neighbor,
beneath the arc light
in the prison cell
where, if there is justice in the land, he will soon end his days.

he thanked his lawyer
and
he thanked his friends
and
he promised to contact them
when he entered the afterlife.

but neighbor, his friends will be waiting
a long time to hear from him. there are plenty
taking that slippery path from chicago to hell.
but there are none,
neighbor,
there are no souls who upon reaching the flaming inferno
make the return trip from the devil's clutches
back up
to
chicago.

iris weaver

chief justice caverly says
he doesn't believe in capital punishment for minors
and for that reason,
leopold and loeb
broke a date with the hangman.

not too many satisfied
with a sentence that lets
two cold-blooded murderers live.

caverly says
his decision holds
with the dictates of enlightened humanity.

enlightened humanity,
now there's something the klan could discuss at their next
cross burning.

sara chickering

first there was the circus,
which esther still jabbers on about.
so when the fair came,
i knew i had to take her.
esther never saw anything like a fair before.
she said the midway reminded her of new york.
and at the age of six,
she knew already that games of chance
were just that.
she felt little affection for the sideshows, furious
at the booth where people took shots at the "nigger's head."

she did like the horse races.
for a while.
but what she loved most was
the livestock.
she wanted the names of the cows:
holstein, guernsey, jersey,
ayrshire, hereford, angus.

she wanted the names of the horses, too,
and the sheep.
she cuddled one little lamb, whispering in its ear that funny way she
     does,
telling the lamb that
she'd be looking for it to come be counted tonight when
she tunneled between her sheets,
and i wouldn't be surprised at all
to hear bleating from her bedroom come midnight
and find droppings down the hall tomorrow morning.

harvey and viola pettibone

harvey says:
how was i to know
they'd be so pushy over a broom sale?
stinking stampede it was, vi.

viola says:
you never will learn, harv.

harvey says:
i thought putting those brooms out for one cent would be good business.

viola says:
twelve women taken to doc flitt, harv,
with cuts and bruises. we'll be
lucky if they don't ask us to cover the doctor bills.

harvey says:
doc flitt wouldn't charge us for that.

viola says:
doc flitt hasn't been too
happy with you lately, harv. you and your klan. he might just
charge us double.

harvey says:
klan will see to him if he does.

viola says:
oh fine, harv. you looking to drive away the
one good doctor we got here?
what happens if you need doctoring?

the two stand facing off, each as stout and solid as a house.

harvey says:
nothing's going to happen to me, vi.

viola shakes her head in disgust
and makes up baskets of food
and a free broom
for each of the women who got hurt.

merlin van tornhout

i was driving to the klan meeting
when i picked up a man, his hood and robe in a paper bag.
we were heading to the same place.
but we hadn't gone far
when he pulled a knife on me
and made me get out.

i never have been out-bullied before
but i thought about that boy in chicago,
that bobby franks,
and i looked at the drifter in my automobile,
and i knew
he would gladly do to me
what leopold and loeb had done to that boy
in chicago.

and i got out.

percelle johnson

halfway across the country,
the body of a polish man was found
hanging in an oak tree.

the sheriff's report ruled the man's death a suicide. they said there
was a bottle of liquor in the man's coat pocket.

but certain neighbors made no secret of the fact that they
were not pleased to have a polish national
in their valley.
night riders beat him up the month before.
the bruises and cuts weren't half healed when the letter arrived
saying:
we're coming for you.
signed, k.k.k.

dang,
young merlin van tornhout is walking everywhere
because he "gave" his car to a klansman.
if the riffraff joining the klan these days
can take the one thing most loved from an awestruck boy,
why couldn't they plant a bottle of liquor
in the pocket of a hanged man?

esther hirsh

daddy says this is the high holidays
and i do need to come with him
to the synagogue
so we can have thinkings about
what we did in the year that did just go by,
and make a plan to do better in the year that is to come.
he says mr. levin is locking up his shoes
for the holiday.
i did ask sara chickering if she will have locking up in the
barn and in the field
and have all the animals and the plants think about
what they did last times and plan for the next times.

sara chickering says,
the animals and the plants are too young for such things
and esther is, too.

daddy says sara chickering is right.
but he says
i still have to come to the synagogue and
have some deep thinkings and talkings to God.

i do have talkings to God and deep thinkings
every day.
but i will come with daddy,
even if i can't go fishing there.

ACT FOUR

leanora sutter

the more time i spend with mr. field
the more i learn.

he never went to school after sixth grade.
he had to work.
and then he went to fight in the civil war
on account of his strong feelings about slavery.
and when he returned, he built
carriages and sleighs.
but what he loved most was to paint them
with little flowers and scenes,
and didn't anyone need to show him how.
just like most things he does,
he sits and thinks about it a while,
till he figures it out.

i wash his dishes in the basin
and he sits at the table,
his bald head the brightest
spot in the room.
he's thin as a broomstick,
gangling tall,
his eyes cloudy.
he holds a palette up close to his face
and then he hawks his shoulders and touches his brush to the
waiting canvas.

i asked if i could look through his paintings
instead of just dusting them.
he said i could have one if i wanted. he said the pickings were

kind of slim these days,
that the best had long gone.
i remember when he offered me the typewriter.
i wondered if someone would say i stole a painting
if i carried one home.

mr. field, i said,
watching as he
    sprinkled a meadow with bluets under a cloudy sun.
we could go out sometime so you could remember things to paint.

i never do like being seen with white folks,
but mr. field is different.
anyway, he said he didn't need to go out.
he couldn't see well enough anyway to make a difference.
besides, he said, he
could just sit down and think about a mountain he once saw
or the end of a forest road
and that was enough.
i guess that comes of being around since civil war days.
i have a lot more seeing to take in
before i can sit down and rest with it.

percelle johnson

got my work cut out for me.
more than 200 negroes
have moved into the state
to build the dam.
i'll have to protect them
from the ku klux.
i'll have to protect them
from themselves.

this job sure doesn't pay
enough.

harvey and viola pettibone

viola says:
harvey pettibone, how could you do such a thing?

harvey says:
they had booze in that hotel, vi. they were breaking the law,
serving liquor.

viola says:
so you go in, dressed in those ku klux nightclothes of yours and you
think you'll save the world from the
evils of drink
by raiding the place and smashing a few bottles?

harvey says:
it felt so good breaking that glass, vi.

viola says:
did it feel $400 good, harv? did it?

harvey runs his hand over the bulge of his belly
beneath the straining vest,
sits down on the steps,
and sighs.

reynard alexander

i did not anticipate
when word of the klan first arrived from the south,
that they'd ever trace their way here to vermont,
but
this is no longer a problem
facing some other community.
the klan is in our homes,
our schools,
our factories, and stores.

it has worked its
fingers through the fabric of the state
and if we do not mend the rents soon,
we'll fall to pieces.

sara chickering

i rest my head against bossie's side
    and the thrush,
    the white rush of milk hitting the pail,
    esther singing in the pear tree beside the barn,
how silent the world would be without cows and birdsong.
how silent my world would be
without esther.

esther hirsh

jerry
the dog that did make me feel happy here first
when i did get my fresh air with sara chickering,
jerry
went away to have the long sleep.

i could have standings upstairs and
call downstairs
things for jerry to do
and he did do what i say.

after i did leave the fresh air of sara chickering the first time
to have seeings of daddy in new york,
jerry had leavings too.
sara chickering says he did go to find me.
sara chickering did have such sad feels when jerry did
leave and i did leave too. she
did ask all people who
do love dogs to bring home her jerry.
but no one had knowings where jerry did go.
then a lady did send a letter from connecticut,
and sara chickering did go all that way to see
if the lady had jerry.

when sara chickering did come to the house in connecticut
she made callings from outside
and jerry did bark all the happy feels in his heart
and sara chickering knew she did find her own jerry.
and he did come home to wait with sara chickering for me.
and when i did come again to stay

and i did bring my daddy,
jerry did come with me every day to the post office
to fetch sara chickering her mail.

but today i did go to the post office without my friend jerry.
i did have to tell my feet every time to make one step
and one step more.
my feet did feel so lonely.

johnny reeves

if a dog dies between night and morning,
neighbor,
it is blamed on the
klan.

reynard alexander

a threat came from the klan, in the form of a letter,
advising me to be careful what i print
and what i say,
or the day would come
when i would not print or
say anything again.

it has come to pass that ordinary,
sensible,
hardheaded vermonters
are entertaining these
kluxers.

but surely the moment will pass,
and the same ordinary,
hardheaded,
folks who invited them in,
will sensibly suggest the klan
pack up their poison
and go.

sara chickering

the president and his wife
will be coming through town soon
on their way to plymouth
to visit the grave of their young son,
taken this year from them,
the same year that brought me esther.

esther hirsh

sara chickering helps me dress up
like i am a goblin
and i do dance through the doors of the schoolhouse
and i do sing a goblin song
in my clothes of green that sara chickering did sew for me.
leanora sutter did dress like a gypsy
and she had sittings by a cauldron
where she did stir the air inside with a big shovel
and she did tell the fortunes to the bob-haired
chatterbox girls
and now they do not have fearings
of being old maids
because leanora did tell them
it would not be so.

the room did have streamers of black and orange.
and owls and black cats and witches on their brooms had flyings
    up the walls.
we did eat of carrot cake and cheese sandwiches and
we did drink pots and pots of cocoa
and i don't ever have rememberings of so much fun.

sara chickering

one of the things i like best about mr. hirsh is
that he didn't move himself up here
thinking how rich he would get
on the backs of some rustic vermonters.

he just came up to keep his daughter happy
and to sell shoes.

.

harvey pettibone

johnny reeves' mother
slipped me a letter
when she came in the store to do her shopping.

i think johnny's in trouble,
she wrote. i caught him with
a schoolgirl, she wrote. he said he was teaching her
about the good book,
but it looked like something different to me.

he's a good son, she wrote,
but he's been awful
quick to anger lately.

i know how important that klan is to my johnny,
she wrote.
maybe you men could see to helping him,
lost lamb that he is,
maybe
you
could lead him back to
god's pasture.

harvey pettibone

we threw johnny reeves
out of the klan.
imagine a grown man
    a preacher
forcing himself on a child.

harvey and viola pettibone

viola says:
what you looking at, harv?

harvey turns from the mirror to look at viola.
would you say my head is small?

viola looks at the enormous
locust stump of a head on harvey's shoulders.

yes, harv, your head is small.

harvey grins.
it doesn't matter, he says. small heads can have
as many brains in them as big heads.
i happen to know i have a very well-filled head.

viola smiles and says:
harvey, that sounds like the reasoning of a man
with a small head.

merlin van tornhout

meeting of the klan
and every man standing
demanding those coloreds, the sutters,
get out of town,
and the hirshes,

worse for the hirshes,

who stained a pure
christian woman
by mixing their jew selves
up with her.

but the shoe man and his kid, they're just living there.

in private, harvey pettibone handed me rat poison
from his store.
pour it in sutter's well,
he said.

but it'll kill them!

no, he said, though
it will make them pretty
sick.
and he didn't look too happy about any of it,
but the exalted cyclops was looking on
so harvey pushed the poison at me.

that's when the roar started inside my head.

johnny reeves

there is only one way
to redeem myself
with my klan brothers.
only one way
to redeem myself
with god.

esther hirsh

someone did shoot my daddy
right through sara chickering's door.
and my daddy did have so much
blood rushing out of him
and sara chickering did leave me alone with my daddy
and i had so quiet talkings to my daddy and
sittings on the floor
next to his poor head
and he did listen to every thing i did whisper in his big white ear
but he had the bad kinds of breathings
and all the blood kept
rushing out of my daddy
and the bullet went clink in
the water pail.

fitzgerald flitt

i was called to see to ira hirsh,
who moved here from new york with his little girl.

i found a soft-nosed rifle ball had passed
through ira's left arm above the elbow,
scratched a two-inch gouge across his chest,
then passed through his right arm
to land in a
waterbucket beside the table.

sara chickering sounded rattled enough
when she phoned from iris weaver's.
sara chickering, who never gets rattled.
    doc, i left him with esther. i'm sure he's bleeding to death.
    hurry.

when i got to sara's kitchen,
she had ira on the floor and she and
esther were holding handkerchiefs tightly to the wounds.

sara said he was sitting at the table after dinner
and in his lap was esther, not leaning back in his arms as usual,
but leaning forward,
studying the crossword puzzle he'd just finished.
someone came onto the porch, so silent, and sara's dog
dead.

the curtain was shut. they must have aimed their rifle
through the keyhole.

why would someone do such a thing?
i asked sara.

klan,
sara answered.

harvey pettibone

viola sleeps,
she is so soft and warm when she sleeps,
and i am silent as i come in
from night riding.

sent a boy to do a man's job.
then i wasn't man enough
to finish it. i never thought it'd come to
this. thought i'd be helping the law,
not breaking it.

viola pats the bed for me to
join her.
she makes room for me in her sleep.

i cannot get in bed with viola.

merlin van tornhout

when i couldn't put the poison in sutter's well,
i went to harvey. he said they'd come after me, the klan would.
i don't have any choice but to run.

sara chickering

esther might have heard the gunman
with those ears of hers,
but she won't talk about it.

how grateful i am that she was leaning forward
over mr. hirsh's crossword puzzle.
if not she would have taken the bullet herself,
straight through,
and she wouldn't be alive now,
clinging to my nightgown,
even as she sleeps.

esther hirsh

sara chickering did feel afraid this morning
to go out and do the milkings
and deliverings of her creams and butters.
i did come out in my chore clothes to help her
and she had smilings for me
and chasings off of her afraid
like a big horse, rolling off the itchings.

it did take a long time
for all the people who wanted to have talkings with us
but we did finally have done all the chores
and i did stay home from school.

percelle johnson

been interviewing people all day,
trying to figure who stood on sara chickering's porch
and fired a shot through her kitchen door.

mr. hirsh is at the randolph sanatorium,
resting comfortably.

how's the child resting i keep asking myself?
how's the person resting who fired that shot?

and where the hell is merlin van tornhout?

reynard alexander

persecution is not american.
it is not american to give the power of life and death
to a secret organization.
it is not american to have our citizens judged by
an invisible jury.
it is not american to have bands of night riders
apply the punishments of medieval europe to
freeborn men.

the ku klux klan must go.

leanora sutter

daddy says:
the k.k.k.
went and burned down the great bethel african church in chicago.

> i feel that old rope of dread
> dragging up the ridge of my spine

daddy, i say,
the klan burns down a negro church in illinois,
they rob a catholic church in burlington,
they try killing a jew right here.
well, they're just giving white folks a bad
name.

giving white folks a bad name, daddy repeats
and he starts to laughing, and then,
i'm laughing, too.
until the laughter turns on us and we are wringing grief,
our faces touching,
our hands entwined.

first time we're right together like that
since mamma's gone.

percelle johnson

i hate calling for help.
but i just couldn't get to the bottom
of ira hirsh's shooting
and i couldn't let go,
especially with things in town the way they
are with the klan.

detective came over from boston, a mr. wood.
it didn't take him long to uncover all the dirty little
things that were going on here,
the letters sent to mr. hirsh
threatening to tar and feather him
if he didn't move out of sara's place.

it was merlin van tornhout wrote those letters.
i thought i knew merlin. he's got some roughness to him,
but i never thought he'd try killing anyone.
especially with that little girl on mr. hirsh's lap.
but merlin disappeared the night of the shooting.
what else can i think?
detective wood says it was merlin for sure.
says he come up on foot around dusk,
peered through the keyhole in the kitchen door,
saw mr. hirsh seated at the table
with esther on his lap.
thought he could get two with one shot.
says merlin fired through the door
as soon as sara left the kitchen to put the dishes away in the pantry.

just doesn't sound like merlin van tornhout.

harvey and viola pettibone

harvey says:
viola, what have you done with my phonograph and records?

viola is silent. she simply hands harvey a thank-you note.

> *it is with sincere appreciation*
> *that we accept these useful gifts.*
> *the residents at the winslow home for the aged*
> *will get such pleasure from your donation of*
> *a phonograph*
> *and fine record collection.*

harvey says:
what did you do, viola?

viola says:
i'm trying to buy back your good name, harvey pettibone.
you with your broom sales
and your liquor smashing
and your klan.
but you don't make it easy.

harvey turns like a slow mule
and lumbers back into the room
where his phonograph once sat.
he touches the table where the feet of the
phonograph left a divet in the lace cloth.

ACT FIVE

leanora sutter

merlin van tornhout couldn't have shot ira hirsh.
i know
because he was here
standing by the well.

i know merlin was here.
he looked straight at me,
i looked straight back.
it happened the same time someone
shot a bullet through
sara chickering's kitchen door.
whoever fired that shot,
it couldn't have been merlin.

johnny reeves

i saw them
in their hoods,
in their robes,
like ghosts.
they were like ghosts. but

it was the klan who
knocked at my door.
who came after me.
why come after me?
i am redeemed.

esther hirsh

they do say that merlin van tornhout
did shoot my daddy.
i think merlin did go on the heaven train
after the bullet did come through sara chickering's door.
no one can see merlin since that night.
he did go like the kittens, and lewis, and my mamma.
but he did not come onto sara chickering's porch with a rifle
before he left on the heaven train.

merlin didn't make a bullet shoot through my daddy.
i know.
i did see who did.

fitzgerald flitt

percelle johnson found
johnny reeves
wandering,
exhausted,
hungry.

he was branded on the back
with the letters
k.k.k.
and was suffering from shock,
unable to give
any
explanation of his condition.

percelle johnson

it's been weeks now
since merlin van tornhout disappeared.
i don't know where he's gone.
darn that boy.

the radio station over in schenectady
broadcast his description.
but it didn't bring him back.
merlin's got family down near boston.
they put the word out on the boston stations, too.
no reply.

we got word that a boy was found,
but it wasn't merlin.
that boy went home to
his true family,
and merlin's still missing.

viola pettibone

percelle johnson found
a baby girl,
two days old,
stuffed in a shoe box,
wrapped in newspapers,
tied with a heavy cord,
and left behind a tree to die.
what is this world coming to?

i always wanted a baby girl.

harv caught me sniffling over the pork chops.
there, there, vi, he said, patting my shoulder with his beefy hand.
there, there.

i wasn't sure whether to laugh or cry.

reynard alexander

thirty years ago
the people of this country
tolerated 200 lynchings a year.

now, though the klan does its best to stir up racial strife,
there have been
only five lynchings reported.

we have antilynching laws on the books.
but that isn't why necks
are less often
swinging in nooses.

it is the people
saying no.

iris weaver

i swear i saw merlin van tornhout yesterday.
he was walking along a back road in plattsburg, new york.
i slowed down, called "hey, merle."
he looked up.
called "hey" back.

i turned the packard around,
even though she was filled with bootleg liquor and i
could have been sent to prison for my kindness.
i turned the packard around and told the boy
his family was undone over his disappearance.
they wanted him home, no matter what.
at least give them word, i said.
the boy denied he was merlin van tornhout and
walked away.

i thought about going straight to the van tornhouts when i
got back in town.
but i couldn't tell the family i saw the boy
without giving out what i was doing in plattsburg.
and sorry as i am to know the worry of the family,
there's some things you just can't do anything about.

reynard alexander

three keys came to me
in a package
postmarked
stamford, connecticut.

the keys were wrapped in
a piece of gray shirting,
snug in a nest
of brown paper.

one key fit the storeroom,
one the back door,
and one started the truck.

i made this set last year
for merlin van tornhout.
so he could work the graveyard shift.

    well, merlin,
    at least you didn't give them to the klan.

leanora sutter

johnny reeves climbed
to the highest point of the arch
of the steel bridge across the connecticut river
and said nothing.
johnny reeves,
who always has something to say to the crowd
stood,
swaying in the air,
silent.
no traffic moved from one shore to the
other while constable johnson
climbed to the top of the bridge
on an extension ladder.
he balanced, 70 feet from the roadway,
trying to talk johnny reeves down.
constable johnson asked
what reverend reeves was doing up there.
johnny reeves looked at him,
said,
i'm afraid of the klan.
and then he jumped
just like that.

esther hirsh

i did go inside the church of johnny reeves
while sara chickering and doc flitt did swap stories outside.
i did go inside to warm my face and talk to God about daddy being shot
and how the bullet
might have had goings through sara chickering or me
or it might have had goings through daddy's heart and
made the living run out of him.
i did go inside the church of johnny reeves
and have talkings with God
about all the good thinkings and feelings that do race around inside me
and that it didn't matter that someone didn't like us
so
much that they did take a gun to kill us
because so many people did like us
and did come to sara chickering's house to help us.
and no one did hear my little talks with God
because no one is supposed to know the
thinkings of little girls
but just the little girl and God.
but i did come inside the church of johnny reeves
because even if i did not tell constable johnson
what i did see,
i can tell God that i saw johnny reeves
that night daddy did get a bullet through him.
and i did think
if i tell God in johnny reeves' own church,
God does know what to do.

fitzgerald flitt

couldn't find johnny reeves' body.
river running pretty fast after the fall storms.
folks say maybe he didn't die.
but the way he hit,
no one could survive.

esther hirsh

sara chickering does bundle me
in my coat and boots
and hat and scarf and gloves.
and i do go down western avenue
knocking on doors,
selling christmas seals
and eating cookies
while sara chickering
does stand outside each door
waiting for me to come back out
so she can bring me safely home.
    she is so funny, sara chickering.
    i have thinkings she is like a hen over the warm eggs
    since i tried to take the heaven train.

but since the bullet did come through her kitchen door
she does jump when a tree cracks,
she does stand and watch me in my bed when
she thinks i am having sleeps
and i pat my bed
and i do say good things to sara chickering
so she can sleep.
i do tell her stories about the animals in the woods
and the animals on the farm
and the animals in the circus
and at the fair.

but i still have wakings and she is watching me in my
sleeps.

iris weaver

senator greene sent a letter to the press
urging every man and woman
to get out and vote for coolidge and dawes.
well, i would have cast my vote without being told.
women have waited far too long for the vote
    to stay out of it now.
but i'll vote for the man *i* choose.
i don't need anyone, not even senator greene,
telling me what to think.

reynard alexander

by the most tremendous majority
ever known in the country
the voters of the united states
went to the polls
and elected a vermonter.

never before has a presidential candidate
conducted himself during the campaign as did mr. coolidge.
he remained in washington
and did the day's work.
he did not make what can be termed
campaign addresses.
he totally disregarded all attacks made upon him
by his political opponents.
he did not even defend himself against
a personal attack on his record.
he ignored all criticism directed either at him
or at his party.
he was the most silent candidate the country has ever seen.
and he won by a landslide.

let the future take note.

leanora sutter

that crazy mr. field.
i've been taking him out for an airing
most days, lately. says he likes the smell outside this time of year.
wood smoke and leaf rot.
we had stopped to rest on the courthouse steps
when three klansmen decked out in their robes came by
with a wreath of flowers for
armistice day.

mr. field, he attacked those klansmen
as they tried placing their wreath for white men
on the courthouse lawn.
he got so worked up
he snatched the wreath
and threw it down the courthouse
basement,
then chased the klansmen away with
his cane,
    made from the timbers of andersonville prison,
and that's the first I knew he could see.
even through those grimy glasses, he had pretty dead aim.

mr. field stood guard at the courthouse
the rest of the evening.
i had to bring him his dinner.
and sit
and eat with him.
right there,
in front of everyone. and wasn't he in the best mood he's been in
for months.

fitzgerald flitt

walked with sara chickering,
and little esther to
rehearsal
of the choral society.

caring for that merry child has changed sara.
she's lost her hard edges.
and that bitter sag to her lips looks almost kind.
and she smiles.

merlin van tornhout

i wasn't home ten minutes
when constable johnson showed up and
brought me in on charges of attempted murder.

i didn't shoot any bullet through sara chickering's keyhole.
the man who works at the jew store,
ira hirsh,
if he got shot,
i didn't do it. i was supposed to poison the sutters' well.
i couldn't even do that.

i should be scared, but i don't care what happens anymore.
i just couldn't run another day.
figured facing the trouble i left behind
couldn't be worse than dodging
the klan preacher,
johnny reeves
     following two steps behind me
     shadow-eyed,
     smelling of river slime,
showing up every place i stopped.

reynard alexander

the secretary of state of vermont
has rejected the application
received from the k.k.k.
to do business here.

good.

merlin van tornhout

if i had done what the klan sent me out to do,
i'd be in jail a long time. but i didn't. i couldn't.
leanora sutter was looking straight at me.

i remembered her
racing that train

and she was still a colored girl
but she wasn't just a
colored girl,
and i couldn't poison her well,
so i ran.

and now instead, I'm accused of doing something worse.
of trying to shoot mr. hirsh.

i wouldn't hurt mr. hirsh.
he gave me galoshes to bring to
my girl, mary, when he heard about her walking halfway across the state,
trying to get back home.

> they were good galoshes.
> mary grinned when she saw them and threw her arms around me.
> they're the ones the girls wear open so they flap.
> mary was so pleased she strutted around the orphanage
> like she was some kind of queen.
> i wouldn't shoot someone who did that for
> mary.

[150]

but i'm not going to jail at all.
leanora sutter came to constable johnson
and told him i couldn't have put that bullet in ira hirsh
because she saw me at her well that night.
constable johnson asked if that was true.

yes, sir, i said.

and what were you doing at the sutters' well?

the klan told me to poison it.

you poisoned the sutter's well?

no, sir, i told him.
i couldn't. that's why i left town.

leanora sutter

a long time ago i wrote miss helen keller
about how maybe we'd be better off
if no one could see.
then nobody would mind about
a person's skin color.
i sent the letter to her when i first started looking after mr. field.
and now, in the mail comes this book,
the world i live in,
and it's signed to me,
to leanora,
from miss helen keller
herself.
i curled right up
and started reading
and my chores weren't even started
when daddy came home.

merlin van tornhout

i keep looking over my shoulder
since constable johnson let me come home.
but the hoods and robes have vanished from vermont.
guess after everything else, when the government threw out the
    klan's petition
they figured vermont wasn't such a good place for them
    after all.
can't say i'm sorry about that.

fitzgerald flitt

there are always those
who think the world is
going to the dogs
and that everything
approached perfection
only in the
good old days.

they say winters today demand less of us,
and summers now are meek.
and yet little has really changed.
those who move away remember
the massive town hall,
the solid stone church,
the imposing brick schoolhouse.
yet when they return after many years,
they find the buildings
though identical in reality,
strangely shrunken in size and majesty
from the impression
memory produced.

to those who swear our young are on the road to perdition
take comfort in this—
every generation
has felt somewhat the same
for two or three thousand years
and still the world goes on.

johnny reeves

i stand in the pulpit.
the round-faced child
listens a moment,
then laughs,
covering her mouth with the tips of her fingers
before she turns and walks out.

esther hirsh

i did give helpings to sara chickering.
we did dip all the keys in oil and put the oil keys in the locks
and then
      openshutopenshut

we did take feathers and we did oil those
and we did move through the house,
out to the barn,
tickling hinges with our oiled feathers.
we did oil every little place but the porch steps.
sara chickering has thinkings that the porch steps
should make creaky creaks.
she says she does like to know when company
is about to call.

harvey and viola pettibone

harvey, have you ever seen anything like it? viola asks,
dancing in harvey's arms
at the grange.

harvey looks up at the lights
swirling around the room
from the new myriad reflector,
the enormous cut-glass sphere suspended from the ceiling,
revolving horizontally while
beams of colored lights
play upon it.

it's like a snowstorm in may, viola, harvey whispers.

and for a moment
viola remembers
why she fell in love with the great mule of a man in the first place,
and all he's done lately to make things right.
and she nuzzles closer
and they dance to joe ladner's orchestra.

merlin van tornhout

found a young buck trapped
between cakes of ice
on the west river.
dogs chased the buck to the water
and it tried crossing the ice jam
but it fell
into a narrow break
between the cakes of ice.
constable johnson came.
we got hold of the buck and
pulled it up
out of the crevice. lord that thing was big.

the buck was too cold to move at first.
it stood on the ice
staring at us. finally
it scrambled to its feet
gave a jump

and plunged back into the same dang hole we just pulled it from.

constable johnson and i hauled it out again.
this time
the buck stayed clear,
beat it across the ice
stopping on the far bank
     taking one last look

before it bounded away through the woods.
it snorted once.
you could hear the echo all through the valley.

leanora sutter

when i saw merlin at the well that night,
i knew he meant no good.
when our eyes met he looked like
he'd been caught in a trap.

i could have come forward and cleared his name from the first.
i could have told that detective from boston.
i could have leveled with constable johnson.

i didn't.
someone had to pay for me being a colored girl in a white world
        i thought.
merlin ought to pay. so i waited.

but then mr. field said,
leanora, no way to pay a debt
by stealing from someone else to do it.

he's pretty smart, mr. field,
for a skinny, half-blind, old white man.

so i told my story to constable johnson,
and told it again inside the courtroom.

funny thing merlin said the other day when i asked him why he
        came back.
i didn't know if he'd talk to me at all.
but he did.
he said he came back to town cause johnny reeves
had been tailing him, showing up in every town he stopped.

should have seen merlin's face when he heard the news
about johnny reeves jumping from the top of the arch bridge.

looked like he'd seen a ghost.

Discussion Guide to
Witness
by Karen Hesse

About the Book

Witness tells the story of the Ku Klux Klan's attempt to re-cruit members in a small town in Vermont in 1924. A young black girl, Leanora Sutter, feels isolated by racial prejudice and her mother's recent death. She is befriended by Esther Hirsh, a younger Jewish girl, whose innocence and natural optimism provide a sharp contrast to the other characters. The Klan's hate-filled message of white supremacy is voiced by Merlin, a teenager, and Johnny Reeves, a minister in the town, who both become members. Other characters — the town constable and the newspaper editor — try to walk a careful line of neutrality until they realize the importance of taking a stand. Storekeepers Viola and Harvey Pettibone represent two opposing reactions to the Klan's methods as they discuss the issue in their own home. Iris Weaver's char-acter reflects a new freedom for women, who had recently gained the right to vote. Over the course of many months, residents are affected in a number of ways by pressures that build in the community, leading up to a climactic moment of violence. In the form of a poetic play in five acts, this series of events is told through the voices of eleven residents of the town. As the characters speak directly to the reader and relate the juxtaposition of acts of hate and love, violence and peace, terror and kindness, they illuminate the full range of human strengths and weaknesses in one small town.

Discussion Points

Characters and Setting

1. Consider the characters of Leanora and Esther. In what ways are they similar? In what ways are they different?

2. What part does Iris Weaver play in the story? What is the importance of her character?

3. Why do we never hear the voices of Mr. Sutter, Mr. Hirsh, and Mr. Field but only hear about them from other people?

4. When does Merlin begin to change his feelings about Leanora? What causes him to begin to fear the Klan rather than be drawn to it?

5. What part do Viola and Harvey Pettibone play in the story? Why do you think we hear their two voices together, while all the other characters speak alone?

6. Discuss the differences among these characters in the way they react to the Klan: Johnny Reeves, Reynard Alexander, Percelle Johnson, Harvey Pettibone, Mr. Field. What does the Klan represent to each of them? What does it represent to you?

7. What is the connection between Sara Chickering and Esther? Why is Sara so protective of Esther? In what ways have Esther — and her father —made a difference in Sara's life? What other characters are changed during the story because of their connection to another person in the town?

Storytelling and Theme

1. Why did the author choose to tell the story in many different voices? How would your experience of this story be different if it were told only from the point of view of Leanora? of Esther? of Merlin? of Sara Chickering?

2. The characters speak in a series of free-verse poems, each having his or her own distinctive voice. What makes this style effective? How is this book similar to, or different from, Hesse's Newbery Award–winning *Out of the Dust*?

3. Esther has a way of speaking that Leanora calls "funny talking." How do these speech patterns affect your perception of Esther? Why did the author choose this particular style for her voice?

4. Sara Chickering says of the Klan: "There's a kind of power they wield, a deceptive authority." What does she mean by a deceptive authority? Why does the Klan burn crosses and hide their identity behind hoods and sheets?

5. Archbishop Desmond Tutu of South Africa has said: "If you are neutral in situations of injustice, you have chosen the side of the oppressor." What does he mean by this? Which characters in *Witness* attempt to remain neutral in this situation? Which of them changes his or her position of neutrality?

6. The American Heritage Dictionary defines the word "witness" as "one who has seen or heard something . . ." or "an affirmation of a fact, statement, or event." Who are the witnesses in this story and what have they seen or heard? What do each of them affirm to be true? Why do you think the author chose this title for the book?

Conflict and Resolution

1. While there are some residents of the town who respond to the Klan's hate message, there are others who find themselves exhibiting newfound courage in resisting the Klan. Which characters do you feel exhibit true courage? What would you do if faced with the Klan's presence in your community?

2. What lessons do we learn from *Witness* about ways to counteract prejudice and mistrust of people who are different from us? How did Sara overcome her prejudices? How did Leanora overcome hers? Will Merlin overcome his? How do you overcome yours?

About the Author

Cheryl Liston

KAREN HESSE was born and raised in Baltimore, Maryland. The year after she graduated from college, she and her husband tent-camped across the United States for six months. When they reached Brattleboro, Vermont, they found the place in which they wanted to settle and have raised two daughters there. Since the publication of her first book in 1991, Karen Hesse has received numerous awards for her work, including a Christopher Medal for *Letters from Rifka* and *Witness*, and the 1998 Newbery Medal for *Out of the Dust*.

A Conversation with Karen Hesse

How did you become interested in writing this story?

In 1997, while returning from a speaking engagement, I spent the last moments of my flight skimming the airline magazine and came across a short piece about the Ku Klux Klan in Vermont in the 1920s. I read the item, shaking my head in disbelief. Back home I wasted no time in attempting to disprove the article, but to my surprise it was correct. I read Maudean Neill's book about the Klan in Vermont, wrote to her about her research, and tried to imagine how I might take this episode in history and craft a compelling story from it.

Did you know from the beginning how you wanted to write it?

No, I hit one dead end after another, so I finally tucked the idea away and worked on something else. A few years later I received an e-mail from my editor with the subject line: "Book Idea?" The message which followed read simply, "Remember *Spoon River Anthology*?" Suddenly the back corner of my brain flooded with light. I had performed *Spoon River* in high school. That was it! The path to the Klan project had been there all along, blazed by Edgar Lee Masters.

How much of the story is based on actual happenings in real life?

I do a lot of research for my books. I borrowed microfilm from libraries across Vermont, reading seven or eight newspapers of 1923 and 1924 to get a sense of how much attention Vermonters paid to the Klan and what other events were going on at the time. One story in Maudean Neill's *Fiery Crosses in the Green Mountains* caught my interest, about a Klan family that had taken in a man and a child. The man and his son were not Jewish but certain people in the community thought they were and told the family they would have to leave the Klan because they were "harboring Jews." Many events in the book were inspired by news articles I came across, but that story gave me the human hook I needed to land the book.

Were some of the voices easier to write than others?

My gut knotted as I wrote from the point of view of characters whose lives were rooted in bigotry. But there were also narrators who made my heart soar. Disabling my censor, allowing each character to speak his or her mind, I have, in *Witness*, attempted to piece together a mosaic of a community giving birth to its conscience.

Other Books by Karen Hesse

Just Juice. Scholastic, 1998
Letters from Rifka. Henry Holt, 1992
A Light in the Storm (Dear America). Scholastic, 1999
The Music of Dolphins. Scholastic, 1996
Out of the Dust. Scholastic, 1997
Phoenix Rising. Henry Holt, 1994
Stowaway. Simon & Schuster, 2000
A Time of Angels. Hyperion, 1995

Books to Compare and Contrast

For adult readers:

Can't Quit You Baby, by Ellen Douglas. Atheneum, 1988; Penguin paperback, 1989

In the Fall, by Jeffrey Lent. Thorndike Press, 2000; Vintage paperback, 2001

The Inn at Lake Devine, by Eleanor Lipman. Random House, 1998; Vintage paperback, 1999

Keeper of the House, by Rebecca Godwin. St. Martin's Press, 1994; St. Martin's Press paperback, 1995

Lesson Before Dying, by Ernest Gaines. Random House/Knopf, 1993; Vintage paperback, 1997

The Secret Life of Bees, by Sue Monk Kidd. Gale Group, 2002

Stranger in the Kingdom, by Howard Frank Mosher. Doubleday, 1989; Houghton Mifflin paperback, 2002

Things Fall Apart, by Chinua Achebe. Astor-Honor, 1959; Knopf paperback, 1994; Heinemann paperback, 1996

For young adult readers:

Bat 6, by Virginia Euwer Wolff. Scholastic, 1998
The tradition of a sixth-grade girls' softball game between two rival towns —narrated in the voice of all eighteen girls on the two teams — is disrupted in the late 1940s by a prejudice born of World War II.

The Brimstone Journals, by Ron Koertge. Candlewick Press, 2001

The Darkest Corner, by Mildred Herschler. Front Street, 2000

Give a Boy a Gun, by Todd Strasser. Simon & Schuster, 2000

Peer pressure, cliques, bullying, and teacher apathy all lead to a climax of violence in one high school of today as told in the voices of many participants and an outside reporter.

Mississippi Trial, 1955 by Chris Crowe. Penguin Putnam, 2002

Nothing but the Truth, by Avi. Orchard, 1991
Many points of view in this documentary novel indicate the various ways of experiencing a conflict when a ninth grader defies his homeroom teacher and everyone suffers the consequences.

The Sixty-Six Dollar Summer, by John Armistead, Milkweed Editions, 2000

Summer Battles, by Ann R. Blakeslee. Marshall Cavendish, 2000
Eleven-year-old Kath and her sister are spending the summer with their grandfather, a minister in Peaceable, Indiana, in 1926, when he is targeted by the local Klan for preaching against their message and for employing a black housekeeper.

To Kill a Mockingbird, by Harper Lee. Harper Collins, 1999, copyright 1960

Set in Maycomb, Alabama, in the 1930s, and told by the young daughter of the town's principled lawyer, Atticus Finch, this classic novel is an enduring story of race, class, justice, and the terrible consequences of prejudice.

The Wave, by Todd Strasser. Dell Laurel Leaf, 1981
Based on a true incident that occurred in a high school history class in California in 1969; a teacher demonstrates to his students the powerful forces of group pressure and their devastating effect on individual rights.

Background Reading

The Christmas Menorahs: How a Town Fought Hate, by Janice Cohn. Whitman, 1995

The Decade That Roared, by Linda Jacobs Altman. Twenty-first Century, 1997

Fiery Crosses in the Green Mountains: The Story of the Ku Klux Klan in Vermont, by Maudean Neill. Greenhills Books, 1989

Hate Crimes, by Laura D'Angelo. Chelsea House, 1999

Hoods: The Story of the Ku Klux Klan, by Robert Ingalls. Putnam, 1979

The Ku Klux Klan: America's Recurring Nightmare, by Fred
J. Cook. Messner, 1989

For teachers and parents:

*The Anti-Defamation League's Hate Hurts: How Children
Learn and Unlearn Prejudice*, by Caryl Stern-LaRosa and
Ellen Hofheimer Bettmann. Scholastic, 2000
*Teaching Tolerance: Raising Open-Minded Empathetic Chil-
dren*, by Sara Bullard. Doubleday, 1996

Internet Resources

www.splcenter.org (web site of the Southern Poverty Law
Center)
www.teachingtolerance.org (web site of the Southern Poverty
Law Center)
www.adl.org (web site of the Anti-Defamation League)
www.facinghistory.org (web site of Facing History and Ourselves)

Audiovisual Resources

Good Conversation: A Talk with Karen Hesse. Tim Podell Productions, P.O. Box 244, Scarborough, NY 10510. Twenty-minute video. Call 1-800-642-4181.

Witness, a multivoice recording by Listening Library, a division of Random House. Two cassettes including an interview with Karen Hesse. Call 1-800-243-4504.

Discussion guide written by Connie Rockman, children's literature consultant and adjunct professor of literature for children and young adults at the University of Bridgeport, Sacred Heart University, and Manhattanville College, and editor of *The Eighth Book of Junior Authors and Illustrators* (H. W. Wilson, 2000).

Critical Acclaim for *Witness*

★ "Stunning . . . haunting . . . memorable . . . What Copeland created with music, and Hopper created with paint, Hesse deftly and unerringly creates with words: the iconography of Americana, carefully researched, beautifully written, and profoundly honest."
— *Kirkus Reviews,* starred review

★ "The voices personalize the history and reveal how events felt to different people . . . it will spark discussion about how such a thing could happen on your street."
— *Booklist,* starred review

★ "Remarkable . . . powerful . . . vivid . . . The small details seem just right. . . . This is much more than a social tract. It's a thoughtful look at people and their capacity for love and hate."
— *School Library Journal,* starred review

★ "This lyrical novel . . . offers insightful glimpses into the hearts of victims, their friends and their enemies."
— *Publishers Weekly,* starred review

"A thoughtful and thought-provoking examination of a national phenomenon on a local level."
— *Bulletin of the Center for Children's Books*

"This lyric work is another fine achievement from one of young adult literature's best authors."
— *Voice of Youth Advocates*

"The story flows quickly and is a good depiction of a community that has allowed the Klan to take over. . . . Well written, interesting to read, character-driven, and historically accurate."
— *The Book Report*

Awards and Honors for *Witness*

The Christopher Award
ALA Notable Children's Book
School Library Journal Best Book of the Year
Publishers Weekly Best Book of the Year
New York Public Library 100 Titles for
Reading and Sharing

To order *Witness* (Hardcover, 0-439-27199-1, $16.95; Paperback, 0-439-27200-9, $5.99) by Karen Hesse, contact your local bookstore or usual supplier. Teachers and librarians may call toll-free 1-800-SCHOLASTIC. Prices and availability subject to change.